Art Now

Richard Lindner

Richard Lindner

ROLF-GUNTER DIENST

8 COLOUR PLATES, 42 MONOCHROME PLATES

 THAMES AND HUDSON LONDON

Translated from German by Christopher Cortis

General Editor: Werner Spies

First published in Great Britain in 1970 by
Thames and Hudson Ltd, London

Printed in West Germany

ISBN 0 500 22010 7

I

During the fifties the Abstract Expressionists in the United States, and the practitioners of Tachism and *art informel* in Europe, dispensed with direct reference to the object; as a reply to this type of art, based on an associative content of mood, Pop art presented a comprehensible figuration. From a superficial standpoint, it may be counted an achievement of Pop that this "urban folk art" forced a return to the object. Pop is city art. It responds to the city's visual stimuli and rearranges them to produce a work of art; in cases where Pop has more significance than mere manipulated reportage – when, that is, it constitutes an autonomous artistic expression – a certain magic attaches to the object, which is thereby transposed into an intermediate field between realistic depiction and visionary figuration.

Pop, like all art, is associative; in it, details and individual objects become generalized prototypes – the part for the whole. In Pop art the individual image, as the communication channel for a particular environmental situation and for its critical reflection in the artist's mind, is expressed, among other means, through artistic detachment; the image defines the picture's terms of reference to the present. The individuality of the artist concerned, as expressed through his particular "handwriting", loses in importance as against the significant selection of the object portrayed. The emotional world is prereflected and taken over by the painter.

Pop art reveals an apparent romanticization of the environment, the world of mass-consumption. Possible social criticism, in the form of a gesture pointing to particular conditions, is relegated to the background. Painterly means are treated ironically, at one remove, and without the enthusiasm of gestural abstraction. Painting and sculpture as such are transposed, in the work of the Pop artists, onto the plane of mere functional technique. The actual execution of the art object is of only secondary importance: the significance of the unsentimental content is primary. The attitude of these artists to their subject matter at the beginning of the sixties was sometimes one of glorification, sometimes one of criticism; sometimes they were concerned with nothing more than the selection of an appropriate subject. In this way they introduced into art a reality transformed by new means.

The work of Richard Lindner should be seen against this background. Lindner, an American, does not belong to Pop, but Pop art was of decisive importance for him. During the Abstract Expressionist period, all types of nonabstract painting were as frequently as not ignored altogether. For this reason, Lindner's work was slow to find a public, and did not in fact find it until there was a general call for firmly defined figuration, and for a kind of abstraction the content of which was no longer to be found in nebulous emotional associations but in concrete figuration.

This artist's work should be viewed in the context of this century's stylistic experience. Lindner was too young to take an active part in Dadaism. He seems to have missed Surrealism; in any case, he had no significant share in this movement, although he still considers that its possibilities have still not been adequately exploited. Nevertheless, Lindner is familiar with these styles, and has been affected by them. In his work characteristic Surrealistic features reappear, though without reference to Surrealist doctrine as such. The occult and dreamlike elements that characterize many Surrealist works appear in his own as a magical atmosphere surrounding a figuration committed to the present.

Lindner has something in common with the Pop artists – namely his exploitation of the uniqueness of the individual pictorial subject. Like the Pop artists, he is committed to the life of the city, from which he extracts significant situations: these are not reproduced literally but individualized, with a claim to general validity. The Pop artists and sculptors make use of stereotyped technical conventions, such as Roy Lichtenstein's grid patterns and primary colors, Andy Warhol's serial reproductions, and Claes Oldenburg's fetishlike large dimensions and conscious misapplication of material; in Lindner's art, the convention changes from work to work. Pop art seems traditionless; Lindner's work is inseparable from tradition. Pop art, as an aesthetic reaction, attempts to draw a line under previous artistic conceptions; Lindner, on the other hand, endeavors to build on traditions, to renew and extend them. He resists the temptation to work in the new technical media used by the younger artists, on the grounds that he lacks the necessary technical experience.

In Lindner's world, visual demagogy is excluded from the outset. He does not attempt to achieve extra-artistic effects through sheer size, or through technical tricks. His media are conventional: oil on canvas, watercolor, and drawing on paper. In the terms of his media – in all of which he is technically perfect – he has succeeded in creating pictures which, by virtue of the neutrality of their approach, concentrate their whole effect on the significance of form and content.

Pop art figurations, or rather the best of them, are remarkable showpieces of the consumer world; Lindner's pictures have achieved no less intensive a degree of contemporary relevance by dealing with contemporary environmental situations. For Lindner, the significance of content, the image concept, the transformed reference to reality are important. He shares with the Pop artists a certain lack of interest in painting as such. Like Pop, his art is an art of ideas. He finds the idea of "art" suspect, too much of an elite affair. What interests him is the idea of the intensification of environmental experience. And this is surely how the artistic process works in his case, from the subject that he finds in his environment, by way of the first sketches, to the finished painting. Thus, Lindner does not regard the visual prototypes of the worlds of advertising, communications, and entertainment as adequate aesthetic stimuli in themselves: they form a point of orientation for his work, which is thoroughly related to its age and avoids imprecise feeling.

The part played by reality in his work anchors each painting in a particular period of time, of which the objects which appear in the painting are characteristic. But Lindner's contemporaneity does not derive solely from the inventory he makes of the visual prototypes of the fifties and sixties. It is apparent also in the handling of the paint, the color, and the formal planning. The color is usually warm and appealing, while the forms are mainly large and simple, varied with small-scale inserts.

Lindner tackles the themes of the world of commercial consumption, mass culture, and mass means of communication indirectly, allowing his individuality to react to them only insofar as these phenomena serve the development of his own iconography. His figurations bear the stamp of the contemporary situations from which they arise, but are not rigidly determined by them; they are autonomous, personal representations. In this way a dialectic of painting is set up. His painting is dichotomous in a positive way — its message is both open and subtle. Even though one may often detect the artist's desire to identify with the cultural stereotypes of our time, the artist's unique privilege is still preserved: the realization, predominantly through his own visions and according to his own laws, of a personal freedom, the privilege of preserving his own individuality within a society that exists in terms of rationalism — an individuality that applies a discriminating sensibility to the critical illumination of social phenomena.

Richard Lindner was born in Hamburg in 1901. He attended the Kunstgewerbeschule in Nuremberg and in 1925 entered the Munich Kunstakademie. From the outset of his career he worked as a commercial artist. When the National Socialists took power in Germany in 1933, he emigrated to Paris, remaining there until the outbreak of war. In 1941 he arrived in the United States totally penniless. He earned a living by working as an illustrator for such magazines as *Fortune*, *Vogue*, and *Harper's Bazaar*; later he taught at the Pratt Institute in Brooklyn. In 1965 he finally gave up his other pursuits and devoted himself entirely to painting.

The influence of European art on Lindner is unmistakable, and his world of ideas has continued to be basically European, although in recent years his work has been increasingly permeated by American influences; the objective style of the "New Objectivity" current in his youth is still visible in the cool, unemotional representation that he now cultivates. His continual confrontation with American painting in New York since 1941 has left its traces, although one may not speak of direct influence. What certainly has been very influential is the general tone of American art today – generous but rigorous execution of the original inspiration, great immediacy and virtuosity in the iconography.

Although Lindner had many friends among the first-generation American Abstract Expressionists, he does not seem to have been influenced by them. His work was at first not properly understood; it was too obstinately figurative, and insufficiently gestural in its impetus. In America the dominant generation of painters for two decades was composed of abstract artists such as Pollock, Rothko, Kline, and Motherwell, whose artistic discoveries were too extensive to allow other important developments to have their full effect. This may have proved of positive value for Lindner's development. His work had time to come to full maturity, and then achieved its full significance at the end of the fifties. Lindner is in any case too much of an individualist to work inside any particular artistic movement, or to react against one. Looking over his work chronologically, one perceives a compulsive sense of direction, whose goals could perhaps only have crystallized over a long period of development and persistent research.

Lindner held an exhibition of his work (at the Betty Parsons Gallery, New York) as early as 1954; but this does not mean that the quality of his work was recognized early: his withdrawn type of painting, despite the significance of his artistic conception, and the timeless quality of his work, lacked those qualities of protest against the past history of art which might well foster early recognition. Lindner himself remarks on the curious fact that the public began to like his work thanks to Pop art – a matter of pure chance, and a sign of the paradoxical nature of the part played by the public in contemporary art.

Lindner's concern with commercial art has helped him toward security in his composition, in which illustrative elements are increasingly lacking. (He still takes pleasure in designing "banners" or a poster such as that for the Festival of Two Worlds in Spoleto.) Like many other American artists, he has incorporated elements of advertising and purely commercial art in his artistic world. At the same time he has always proved able to use the tricks of the commercial artist's trade in such a way that they reinforce the painterly content of his pictures. His approach also guarantees that these elements are not used in such a way as to consciously and calculatedly form a patterned pictorial disposition. Pop artists have always been quite rigorous in their determination to strip the artistic act of false romantic ideas, and Lindner's method has been similarly sober – idea, theme, sketch, preparatory drawing, and final version – but, unlike them, he has always retained the sublime nuance, the manipulation of color values and formal pattern in terms of his theme.

Lindner's works are not a serial entity: he creates a new iconographic code for each work – thus each becomes a world of its own. This is another contrast with the work of other American artists – for example Robert Indiana's *Lion* and his numeral pictures, Barnett Newman's *Stations of the Cross*, or Andy Warhol's Idol series. Lindner endeavors to grasp his environment as a whole; accordingly, each picture deals comprehensively with a single aspect of a visionarily alienated reality, and at the same time touches on universal problems.

Within the total design, interpretation and representation of the motif take effect in mutually complementary versions. The result is never a planned approach to a complex whole through variation and repetition. The individual pictures describe objects in their own terms and in Lindner's own terms. Lindner thus avoids formal mannerisms and a stiffening or weakening of the figurative typology. The pictures are distinguished by the uniqueness of their stylization and the significance of their poetic interpretation. Lindner, thus seen, is a painter between epochs, conscious of the events in art history which he has witnessed, and conscious of the present, to which he always pays due tribute. The painter's works are not snapshots of social situations in which he participates: he crystallizes what he can use in terms of painting from these situations, uses them as motifs, and creates a concept of creative activity which has proved unique in recent American art. Lindner answers aesthetic radicalism with the total realization of his free imagination. His formal language is innovative in that it combines various forms of stylistic experience and goes on to expand the material through the individuality of the content.

The Surreal alienation of the human environment – a concrete representation of the power of the imagination – involves a dialectical process which precludes any concern with public acclaim; it reminds one, rather, of the dedicated work done in a laboratory. Lindner attempts to deal with the problems of his own experience: the individual presence within the work. He is able, however, to forge a bond between his artistic personality and the public in such a way that his creative message exists within a framework of understanding which retains its own value over and above the relevance of the particular theme: this value is based on the realization of the picture as an aesthetic demonstration. Ambivalence is a necessity both to fill out thematic significance and to validate the formal-aesthetic completeness of the work. Even if this ambivalence is not part of the initial conception, it nevertheless always recurs. The open and concealed elements of his figurations together, without degenerating into a mere intellectual puzzle, lead the observer to explore the thematic frame from his own viewpoint.

Lindner has opened up the significance of the world of the city as it is sociologically manifested through particular phenomena. These manifestations do not appear as stereotyped symbols in his pictures, for he has invented a phantasmagorical heightening of effect; it derives from his use of exaggeration, a language more allusive than mere reportage, preferring reflection to impartial quotation, and experience to fiction. Though this heightening of effect may seem unreal, it has a stronger presence than reality itself, enabling the observer to achieve recognition by overpowering him with symbols of meaning. Lindner continually creates a connection with reality, not by means of the shock effects of Surrealism, but through the witty intensification of artistic situations. The prototypal significance that adheres to his figures constitutes a further connection between the reality of the picture and that of life as it is experienced.

The unforced painterly delicacy, the clear formal progression within the area of a painting, and the poetic suggestive power that his work possesses, all give Lindner's oeuvre its special position within midcentury painting. Like the Pop artists, Lindner takes as his theme the banality of the environment and, without losing any of its significance, transposes it into a new context of form and content: he does this so successfully that the specific moment in history when these pictures were made can be pieced together like a mosaic. In his later work, this reflected environmental experience is so strong that the artistic imagination becomes identical with the picture of reality that it filters and processes.

From its beginnings, Richard Lindner's work has had components of caricature, achieved through the stylization or conscious overdrawing of his figures. In his later work the use of strong, unrealistic color adds to this effect. Although the foundations of his career were laid in Europe, the works that have been preserved are almost exclusively from his American period. Those that date from 1950 to the present can be chronologically documented. The changes in his paintings succeed each other cautiously, and the forms of his painting since 1960 can be seen to have originated in his earlier work.

The portrait of Marcel Proust (*pl. 1*), a small oil painting dating from 1950, is a characteristic work, not only from the point of view of physiognomic decoding – the face is stiffened like a mask, pale, hollow-eyed, and introverted – but also because it contains an element often found in Lindner's later paintings, namely, clothing as a kind of protective shell. In the Proust portrait this element consists of the high collar surrounding the writer's neck like armor; the coat also has the quality of a protective, defensive "packing". Clothing is often the index to a particular situation in Lindner's work, and reflects the various epochs that the artist has treated. In his pictures dating from the fifties, he has clearly been influenced by the period before World War II. The personality of the figures in them is always visible through the assemblage of suits, costumes, and so on, which are always presented with painterly reserve. *The Visitor* (1953, *pl. 5*) shows a male figure in the background, frozen in the elegance of tails and top hat, waistcoat and stick. As in other portraits of the period the face is doll-like – round, healthy, and chubby. This figure is balanced by the young blonde girl in the foreground; her posture is youthful and carefree, and is further emphasized by the colored hoop and sailor suit. The arrangement of the figures is carefully calculated. The doorway sets off the figure of the gentleman; the girl's head is emphasized by the red wall behind. Both figures have a certain mechanical quality, and the whole picture looks like a snapshot. The painting here becomes smoother, more emphatically *trompe-l'oeil*, and the tones of the colored forms are more illusionistic than in Lindner's earlier work.

One of the most important of Lindner's early pictures is *The Meeting* (*pl. 3*). This picture dates from 1953, and is relatively large in format. Now in the possession of The Museum of Modern Art in New York, it shows a group of nine figures. All the factors that are later to become so important in his works are contained in this one painting. The figures are a retrospective cross-section of the artist's family and friends – including such persons as Hedda Sterne, Saul Steinberg, and the photographer Evelyn Hofer. The group of women seems to represent a process of maturation. The scale extends from the schoolgirl in her sailor suit, by way of the worldly young beauty, to the cool, experienced-looking matron. In the first row are to be found a sad-looking young woman; a figure representing King Louis II of Bavaria; a girl in a corset seen in rear view; a giant cat; and a man wearing a hat who sits stiffly on a chair. King, cat and corseted girl, in particular, are elements that one will encounter in Lindner's later works. The figure of Louis II, with its sensual lips, somewhat conceited air, accurately painted fur, wing collar and hypertrophied limbs, is a type that recurs. The figure of the girl with the elaborate corset and the large garters is typical of Lindner's figure presentation, the statuesque block-shaped limbs contrasting with the comparatively delicate body. Like Louis II, the great glaring cat also seems to have been incorporated into the picture as a symbol. All these three elements are particularly distinguished by their monumental, sculptural characteristics.

Lindner's drawings and watercolors usually accompany oil paintings. They filter the theme, even if it appears slightly changed in the final version in oils. What is striking about his work is his wealth of artistic nuance. The figures and objects are progressively contoured and modified. Transparent overlays of color serve to accentuate the various spatial levels, the front and back, the various shapes that overlap and intermesh. His drawings are less linear than three-dimensional. One example of this is *The Corset* (1954, *pl. 2*). The picture is dominated by a massive female figure with a charming little head. The figure is subject to a strict architectonic scheme. The arms are opening the outer layer of the corset. Once again this feminine accessory appears as a form of armor. Moreover, the strict lines of the room's perspective contrast with the soft, smooth, rounded forms of the woman, whose dominant pose makes her appear monstrous. Here, as in his paintings, Lindner's concern is not with naturalistic presentation, but with alienation through distortion, selective accentuation and spatial illusion. A seemingly realistic representation blends with Surrealist heightening of effect. The room tapers upward – as does the female figure – following a logical perspective and forming a spatial contrast to the presence of the woman.

In the period from 1954 onward, monumentalized single or double portraits alternate with figures accompanied by a puzzle-type organization of forms. In *Boy with Machine* (*pl. 7*), an oil painting dating from 1954, a concrete object, in which complex articulation of form acts as a dialectical antithesis to the monumental figure, takes the place of abstract formal interpolations. The boy's figure is set in the center of the canvas, as so often in Lindner's work, and the lower half of the boy is oversized. The legs are statuesque and thick. The feet, in buckled shoes, are huge. The hands and the head are much more delicately treated; the fingers hold a spindle and a rope, which are part of the complex machine appearing in the background. The levers, wheels, and cylinders of the machine combine to make a complicated formal pattern. The child's face expresses joy in play. The shining, obviously functional machine seems to possess a threatening power. The boy is characterized by simplification of form, although there are spatial subtleties. *His* nature is open and direct, while the function and the power of the machine remain unknown, concealed by the complicated arrangement of its parts.

The Billiard (*pl. 8*), begun in the same year and completed in 1955, is clearer in its arrangement of figures. Two male figures dominate the left and right of the picture. In the center the main feature is the billiard table, with a striking red ball: the background is once again a mere suggestion of architecture. The table and billiard cues produce mutually intersecting lines of movement. The players are elegantly dressed, and the painter has taken great pains to render their costume accurately. The colors are kept dull, to produce the effect of a certain neutrality of mood: they also convey something of the concentration and tension of the game. Two further works dating from 1955 are characterized by clear compositional articulation of the canvas. *The Couple* (*pl. 6*), a vertical work, is divided into two sections by strips of color. The top section presents a naked man, the bottom section a naked woman, each figure being set centrally in its area of color. Symmetry is disturbed by a disk beside the man's head, by a geometric pattern above the woman's head, and by a vertical strip of color in the lower section. The male figure is sinewy and muscular, and shows a certain toughness. The peaked cap gives the naked body a stiff, military quality. In contrast to this, the female figure has more rounded planes and is more ingratiatingly presented: the flow of the contours is gentle; the hair is waved; one hand gracefully extends a finger. Were it not for the graphic arrangement of the figures and of the geometrical ornaments, the painting would almost be realistic.

A second work with the same title (*pl. 9*) is more illusionistic in style; this is an oblong picture in which the spatial arrangement of the objects depicted is Surreal in quality. Abstract geometrical shapes divide up the canvas. The male figure appears as a bust in profile, with a wig and medieval clothing. The profile is sharp, with a large nose, double chin, and hard mouth. The figure radiates a despotic quality. The female figure is of a different era, wearing a cap and a dress which reflects partly organic, partly mechanical shapes; she is set off to the right side of the picture, and stands before a flat background. The composition is comprehensible and clear. The male head is placed in the upper left section of the canvas along with the geometrical shapes; below this is a table on which is a box, cut off by the left-hand edge of the picture, and on the right is the dominant female figure. Lindner has dispensed with densely packed detail: the whole area of the picture is strictly articulated by means of separate figures and abstract forms, powerful expanses of color and sharply defined contours. As in the earlier picture on the same theme, everything is linear and large-surfaced, and spatial associations are used very sparingly.

Subsequent pictures up to 1959 are more complex and compartmented. Space is intricately assembled with an almost Cubist articulation; the individual figurative parts of the pictures are emphasized in isolation against a background of abstract forms. Not until 1960 does Lindner return to more explicit compositions; indeed, between 1955 and 1960 the expressive content of his representation of the human form remains more or less constant. The female figure is the single dominant factor, and corsets constantly recur as complicated structures – for example, in *Woman in Corset* (1956, *pl. 10*), *The Entry* (1958, *pl. 14*), *Stranger No. 1* (1958, *pl. 17*), and *The Target* (1959, *pl. 41*). The figures in these pictures play a less dominant role than in the works of 1950–55, even though the abstract formal structure constantly recalls them and uses them as a basis for development. These figures – as in *Woman in Corset* – are split up into ridged areas of aggressive effect, then are recomposed into torso-like bodies. In *The Entry*, the main feature to appear out of the intricate complexities is a corset. Effects of movement, spatial disorientation, and formal division are achieved by means of sharp-edged and rounded parts, dotted lines, and the emphatic figurativeness of individual sections. The manifold complexities and combinations throughout the whole picture lead one to dissect it. Not until *Stranger No. 1* and *The Target* does the figurative architecture again become dominant. The figures – in *Stranger No. 1*, man and woman; in *The Target*, a female figure and a dark, mechanical silhouette – stand out clearly from the background. What is retained from previous works is the free pictorial composition, the interpolation of badge-like forms, and the interplay between individual parts of the body and small abstract shapes. However, increasing emphasis is placed on the characterization of the human being. The woman in *The Target* is once again monumental, unyielding and aggressive through the strength she consciously displays. The legs form a pillar-like foundation for the lacing of the corset. The one breast which can be seen is bare, as in nearly all of Lindner's female figures, and is painted in the form of a disk. The various circular shapes – kneecap, breast, target, and ornamentally disposed circles behind the woman's left hand and within the dark-toned silhouetted figure – balance the splintered areas of the canvas, which have the effect of figure dissection.

In the oil paintings dating from 1958 to 1960, intricately compartmented surfaces are still present, but the figurative areas are more clearly stressed than before. The heads and the bodies of the human figures are quite clearly distinguished from the abstract spatial and surface divisions. The combinations of wedge-shaped planar formal components are cumulative in effect. They create a powerful contrast to the heads and bodies of the human figures. This is very noticeable in *One Afternoon* (1958, *pl. 12*), which shows a girl in profile and a boy in full-face, both surrounded by plane segments that certainly have some reference to the total composition but cannot be seen in connection with the two children.

Stranger No. 2 (pl. 15) is a picture of considerable significance. Here the contrast between human and abstract forms is less marked; the abstract forms are arranged like statuary, sharply contrasting with one another in terms of color and shape, and seem to illustrate the transformation of the human being into a machine, a functional, obedient apparatus. Herein a critical aspect makes itself felt – as it will even more strongly in the paintings that follow. Man is no longer seen within the safety of the idyll, but exposed to a threatening and dangerous environment, one against which he reacts, but to which he also adapts. An example of this may be the stranger in this picture, a prototype of the human being as taken over by the technical age.

In 1960, Lindner's compositions become clearer and more lucid. The individual segments no longer intermesh but stand side by side; in addition, they are more strongly contrasted, through the increasingly violent use of color. Abstract forms are more delicate, and often are sparsely strewn in larger areas, in order to interrupt them and give them more life. In *The Target No. 1 (pl. 27)* the face of the male figure is broken up by compartments of color in a "gestural" abstract style, in the center of the painting. This is divided into two vertical halves: on the left is the darker section, which encompasses part of the male and the female figure below it; the right half, lighter in tone, is spread with abstract signs, a coil shape, and geometrical forms developing from the edge of the canvas. The woman's head is seen in profile: its composition has a closed and total validity of its own, and its expression indicates a self-confident dominance. The male figure is divided up into sequences formed of self-developing circular segments: these are combined and completed by a hat. A discontinuous distribution of the figures over the canvas was already characteristic of the horizontal version of *The Couple (pl. 9)* in 1955. In *The Target No. 1* the figures grow out of the lower edge of the canvas.

This theme of illusionistic space is taken up again in *The Secret* (1960, *pl. 25*). A girl and boy seem to penetrate into the central area of the painting from the canvas edge. The movements are cut off and separated by spatial differentiation. The clothing of the two children at play is once again complex and armorlike, the legs heavy and coarse, the heads small. The girl is swinging a rope with gusto: behind the rope's contour appears a ball-like shape. An observer watches the two children's activities from above, his cheek pensively resting on one hand. All that is visible of this spectator figure is the arm, hand, and one half of the face, the rest being concealed behind a towerlike shape that pushes its way into the picture. Although in subsequent paintings the earlier theme of juxtaposed fragmentary forms constantly reappears, the pattern shown in this picture remains typical of most of Lindner's following work. It has an effect of steely precision, owing to Lindner's use of strong but cold, emotionless color. A spatially ambivalent sensation is created by the form, and this, too, is intensified by his use of color.

Lindner's next paintings have an increasing number of scenes connected with play and amusement; historical figures also appear, as do couples, and individuals who appear to be threatened. Coney Island, the New York recreation center and super-fairground, is the theme of the picture of the same name dating from 1961 (*pl. 33*). The powerful figure of a man with hat, mustache, and stick is seen against a background consisting chiefly of primary colors. His jacket is colorfully faceted, as are his waistcoat and face. The color radiates gaiety; the mood is genial, and is emphasized by the man's clownish appearance. *Musical Visit* (*pl. 23*), painted in the same year, has a similar formal arrangement. This picture is again characterized by appealing color, with strong accents of red, but is more complicated in arrangement. A stiff male figure is surrounded by organic and geometrical shapes, among which a vertical piano keyboard is especially conspicuous. In another painting, *Two Faces* (1961, *pl. 22*), the human face is again distorted by extreme color emphasis. A dog with bared teeth moves into the canvas from the bottom right-hand corner. The facial expression of the male figure (the profile and full-face view blend) is frightening. One's attention is directed to this unnerving double-facedness by means of a segment of a circular ring, divided into various color zones. Once again, a complex geometrical scheme is contrasted with clear divisions by means of wide areas of color.

Use of ornament to give life to individual sections of a painting is even more extensive in *Solitary III* (1962, *pl. 30*). A female figure is framed by two clearly contoured male figures, which partially conceal the patterned screen before which the female figure stands. Against the coarse stature of the men, the woman has a coquettish erotic effect, evoked not least by the fragility of the XVI figure's arrangement. She seems to stand between the two men in an ambivalent way, offering and yet withholding her charms: her attitude seems playful, but is not without a certain aggressiveness.

From 1962 onward, the composition of Lindner's paintings becomes considerably clearer, although continued use is made of functional filling-in shapes, geometrical patternings, and badge-like signs, in order to animate and enliven various areas of the canvas. The expression and conception of the figures harden increasingly, and they are more freely interspersed with stereotyped elements. Two paintings dating from 1962 illustrate this very well. These two works – *Louis II* (*pl. 24*) and *Napoleon Still Life* (*pl. 25*) – contain historical references. Both vertical canvases, they display heavily stressed, dominant male and female physiognomies.

The figure of Napoleon, sharply contoured like a paper cut-out, is robustly conceived; the mouth is hard, and the inflexible eyes and jutting chin further emphasize the energetic expression. In *Napoleon Still Life* the geometrical forms are surmounted by the bust of a woman. Her unchangingly dominant role is indicated by a two-section coiffure, the historic and modern hairstyles underlining her enduring power. Especially noticeable are the eroticism of her wide, sensual mouth, and her searching, enticing expression. The compact composition and the energetic expression of the faces complement the large areas of color; the cockade is a key to the picture's theme, as are the initials "L. 2" in *Louis II*. In previous paintings the monumental ambiance of individual figures dominated each picture. In these works, the generous expanses of color and the directness of the objects complete and unify the effect. In the course of less than two decades Richard Lindner has achieved an increasingly clearer and more decisive use of formal means without ever deviating into formalism; aim is not merely to reflect his own psyche, but to speak a universal language.

Lindner has always been keenly interested in the alteration of the human identity by means of clothing. The conscious theatrical unreality of his figures is achieved not only through the treatment of the individual physiognomy, but also through the use of such accessories as hats, spectacles, suits, coats, and costumes; of no less importance is the action which takes place within the picture itself. A good example is *The Actor* (1963, *pl. 28*). The actor's face, adorned with waved hair, bushy eyebrows, and neat mustache, is so expressive in its distortion that it seems to reflect only one moment. The combination of bow tie, leopard skin, and tail coat forms a varied, diffuse costume that puffs out the wearer. The formal arrangement of the clothing follows the dramatic expression of the face, as does the curved and mobile design of the background.

In *119th Division* (*pl. 31*), a painting completed in 1963, a massive woman appears, fully equipped with fashionable accessories and having a sly expression. She radiates conscious femininity – as in fact do all the females in Lindner's recent paintings. The picture is divided up into an elaborately detailed front view of the woman and a silhouetted, mysteriously diagrammatic side view.

In Lindner's paintings, women tend to conceal their identity less than the male figures do. This is clearly demonstrated by the scenery in *Coney Island No. 2 (pl. 39)*, painted in 1964 – an especially productive year for Lindner. Man and woman are here enclosed by a badge-like circular shape. The movement of the female body is exciting and dynamic. Her bodice is decorated with a black panther, her shorts are striped. She seems to be rushing toward the black-masked man. The woman is presented as a typical American, whereas the man remains a generalization: both figures are nevertheless linked by a mysterious attraction.

The theme of New York's amusement centers, already represented in the two Coney Island pictures, recurs in *42nd Street (pl. 55)*, which focuses on the Times Square district. The symmetrically laid-out painting shows two full-face heads of a blonde woman and two profiles of a man. The whole composition is arranged like a gaming "fruit machine" around these heads: brightly colored balls form arcs and strips of color, a tiger growls threateningly, and stripes, circles, and angled geometrical elements provide a many-colored juxtaposition. The male and female figures are characterized as types found in this area of New York by elements such as the woman's heavy make-up. The woman is seductive and disturbing. In this picture Lindner has succeeded in producing one of his densest and also most accurate summaries of a section of American life. The noisy streets, the harsh lights of Times Square, the atmosphere of bars and gambling halls, seem to manifest themselves simultaneously.

This directness of language is also found – though with certain nuances – in a series of watercolors painted in the same year, 1964. Examples are two versions of *New York City (pls. 35, 37)*, *Woman with Handbag (pl. 50)* and *The Target (pl. 41)*. In the New York series Lindner effectively documents the people of the big city. The men are calculating and cold. The women are sphinx-like, ambivalent beings, whose disguise serves their ends. Woman is often portrayed by Lindner as monstrous and dangerous. In this connection reference is often made to his studies in Nuremberg – that ancient medieval city with its fierce Gothic architecture and its Iron Maiden. Lindner's portrayal of woman as a mysterious, tyrannical, compelling figure is emphasized by the clothing in which she is presented – leather accessories, whips, boots, caps, and something closely resembling folk costume. However, many factors also underline the female's inherent humanity; for example, in the superb watercolor *Woman with Handbag*, the complex accoutrements become a sort of armor, within which the woman radiates her dynamic presence.

In 1965 Richard Lindner became guest professor at the Hochschule für bildende Künste in Hamburg. There is, however, no record in his work of this encounter with the city of his birth. In Hamburg he painted the large *Disney Land* (*pl. 44*), a representation of the glamour and hedonism of American, and especially Californian, culture. California and New York are two points of orientation for Lindner's view of the American way of life. He has often been inspired by the turbulence of the city and its complex spread of amusement areas. The icecream-licking, short-skirted girl poses in front of the luminous "Disney Land" sign, which in turn is combined with a slot machine. The mechanical nature of the environment is suggested by a brightly painted parrot's head, the numbers of the machines, and a flurry of stripes. A similar girl appears in *ICE* (*pl. 46*), a work of the following year. Her statuesque figure is seen framed in a rhomboid shape: she, too, is eating icecream. The hands are gloved, the legs are clad in gaudily striped stockings, and the face is partly obscured by spectacles and helmet. The hair flows over the shoulders and breasts. The abdomen is covered with a star bearing an Indian's head. Here, too, the figure of the American girl is erotic and domineering.

In 1965 Lindner painted yet another female double portrait (*pl. 43*), which also marks a stylized female type. The head appears beneath a helmet-like hat, and the eyes are hidden behind fashionable sunglasses. The upper part of the body is clad in armorlike layers, only the neck and cleavage remaining free; the breasts jut out like proud emblems. The bosom, mouth, and heavy body characterize an individuality that hides itself in order to be more enticing.

Apart from *ICE*, there is the series of large paintings that Lindner produced in 1966 for a show at the Cordier & Ekstrom Gallery in New York. Among them are the Beatle portrait *Rock Rock* (*pl. 54*), *Leopard Lily* (*pl. 47*), *Telephone, Hello,* and *Pillow* (*pl. 45*). His slow and meticulous method has prevented Lindner from producing a great body of work, but this means that the presence of each individual work is all the stronger. His themes all involve the relationship between man and woman: his presentation of the female is the more intense of the two. Moreover, many of his paintings show that Lindner has been fascinated by the assertive, perhaps even dominant role played by women in American society. His women often resemble idols, to which the artist's attitude is at once reverent and critical.

The female figures of his recent years appear increasingly youthful, like the apparitions of the film and entertainment world. The gaiety, stylization, and inventiveness of youth are expressed in the large works, such as *Leopard Lily* (*pl. 47*) and *ICE* (*pl. 46*). *Rock Rock* (*pl. 54*), showing a long-haired youth with a guitar in front of a broadly striped background, is a tribute to the sixties.

In 1967 Lindner produced a series of prints and a "portrait" on the theme of Marilyn Monroe, who became an American idol to a greater extent than almost any preceding actress. Lindner presents her in the colors of death; a great, towering, partly black statue, she is feminine and mysterious; the portrayal is signal-like in formal disposition and appealing color. A watercolor, *Marilyn Was Here* (*pl. 53*), formed a study for this work, but differs from it in the use of collage elements and in the complexity of figuration. The collage elements are a garter, pieces of flag, part of a photograph of Monroe, and the printed letters which form the title. Lindner's artistic vision is that of an interpreter of human relationships in our age. This shows itself above all in the large paintings of recent years. Without dispensing with the full working out of his themes in paint, Lindner has made his later paintings still simpler and compositionally clearer to interpret. His other works are confined to colored drawings, watercolors, and gouaches, mostly produced in connection with the oil paintings. Lindner enjoys the directness with which he is able to express himself on paper, the spontaneous notation of his figurations with colored pencil or watercolor brush. In these works his outlines are more seismographic, and the figures more finely worked out, than in his oil paintings, which are designed to achieve an effect of monumentality.

Lindner often works out his preliminary ideas on paper. Even though he has recently taken to using a projector for visualizing his sketches on canvas, Lindner has still remained faithful to the "academic ritual" of painting. Frequently he works from models, and from photographs and reproductions as well. Nevertheless, in spite of all his prior planning and calculation, his figures radiate a directness and freshness that reveal the spontaneity and ambivalence of his imagination. This being so, each aspect of his work — whether drawing, watercolor, or oil painting — is as important as any other, for it has required the same intensity of artistic effort.

Printmaking occupies a relatively unimportant place in Lindner's work, even though he had ample opportunity for work in this field during his years at Pratt Institute. He has produced a few lithographs and silkscreen prints, and also, in the form of a "multiple", a banner on felt with simple forms printed in clear, strong color; these few prints by Lindner (most of them made in the sixties) show his personal style, and his brilliant gift for formal invention, just as clearly as does the rest of his work. His reserve in respect to the print may seem all the more surprising in view of the fact that Lindner worked for long periods of his life on graphic design, chiefly posters and illustrations. But his predominant concern is not with any particular technique as such; rather, it is with the use to which he can put it in realizing his artistic conceptions.

Lindner's oeuvre seems clearly defined, yet still open to new formal findings that will serve his imaginative world. From the very beginning, his work shows a consistency of thematic mood: this achieves full clarity of formulation only in his later work. The particular problem of theme is not a closed or static affair, however; it remains open to the changing phenomena of the age. Seen thus, his pictorial world is one arrived at after the artist has used his own experience as a basis for testing, filtering, and orienting his theme. He has been able to give such visual shape to his imagination that his personality always remains perceptible; yet the figuration never becomes the kind of manic self-presentation in which only wishes and compulsions can take shape.

Lindner's work is characterized by fetishism, eroticism, projection of an image in the context of his time, and commitment to – and reflection on – city life and its phenomena. The past – as in the tragic figure of the Bavarian King Louis II, or in the portrait of Napoleon – and the present, with its ambivalent terms of reference, become comprehensible in his work in a personal way. Although his interpretations are quite individual in style, the emotional neutrality of a Léger and a Surrealist tendency to combine thematic elements are basic to all his work. His painting does not become identifiably "American" until the later years, through themes taken from mass culture and also through harder use of color plus decisiveness of form. Though his paintings must be viewed in the context of modern American painting, they still have their own individual language, which is not confined to the environment that serves as their point of origin. The poetic magic which emanates from these works is accompanied by a menacing monumentality of style. The paintings bring together the bourgeoisie and urban extraversion. The earlier works are comparatively serene; the later paintings shift into declamatory postures. Lindner's work is characterized by reminiscences of medieval cruelty and by the implacable reduction to stereotypes which is a feature of the culture of today's big cities.

Lindner's work is distinguished by so personal a vision that it escapes generalized stylistic labeling. The artist's personal experience – a youth spent in Germany, persecution by the National Socialists, life in the New World – has found documentation in an oeuvre that has actualized and interwoven the stylistic phenomena of the twentieth century in such a way that his personal imprint remains legible. Lindner's contribution to art is outside the boundaries of opportunist stylistic radicalism, and is wholly committed to imagination and to its meaningful concrete expression.

1

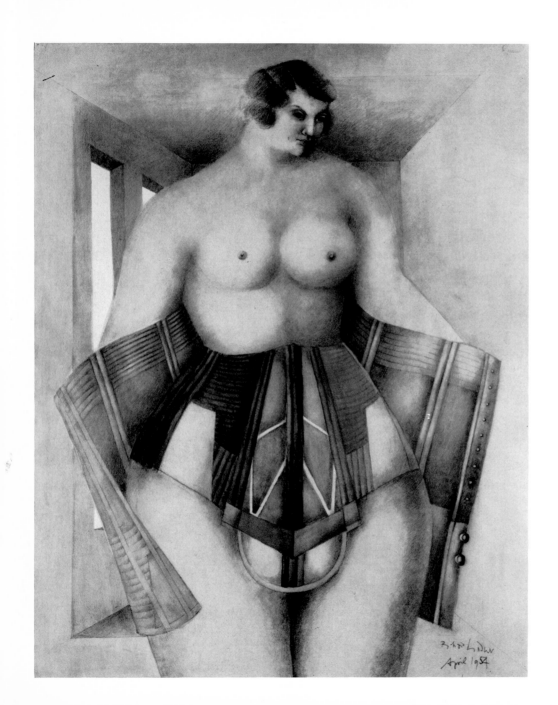

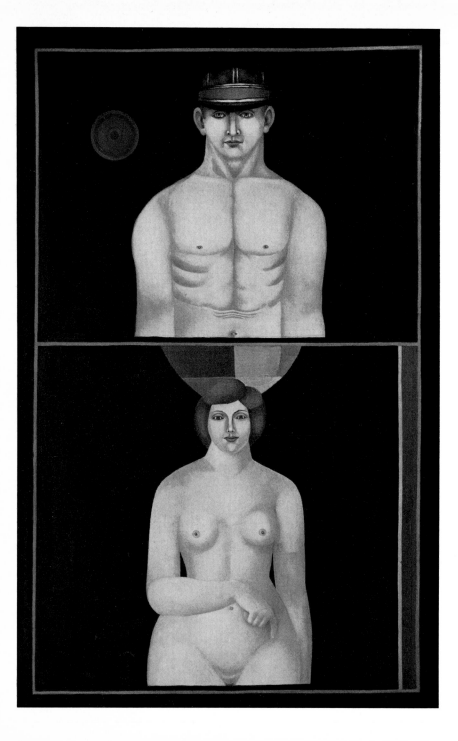

6

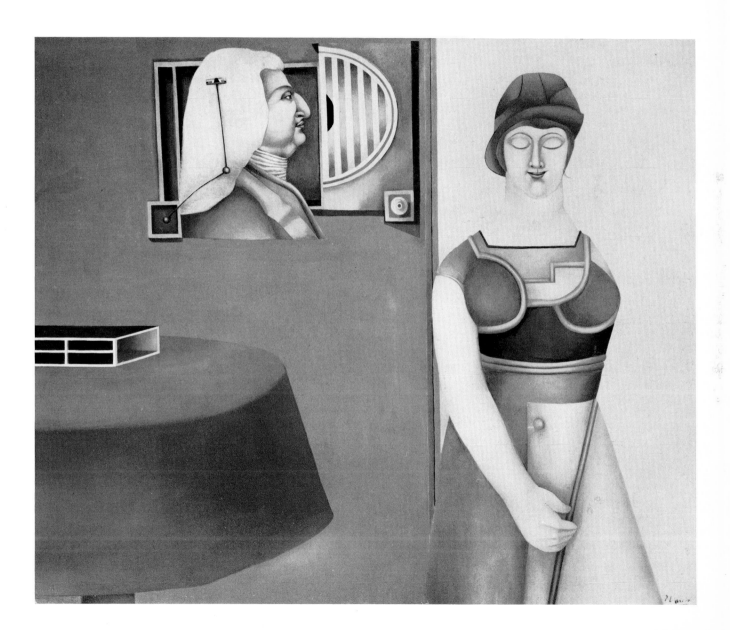

9

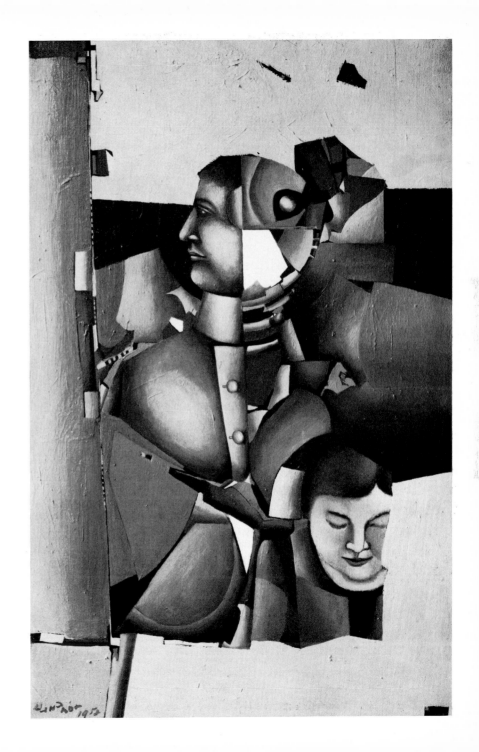

12

14

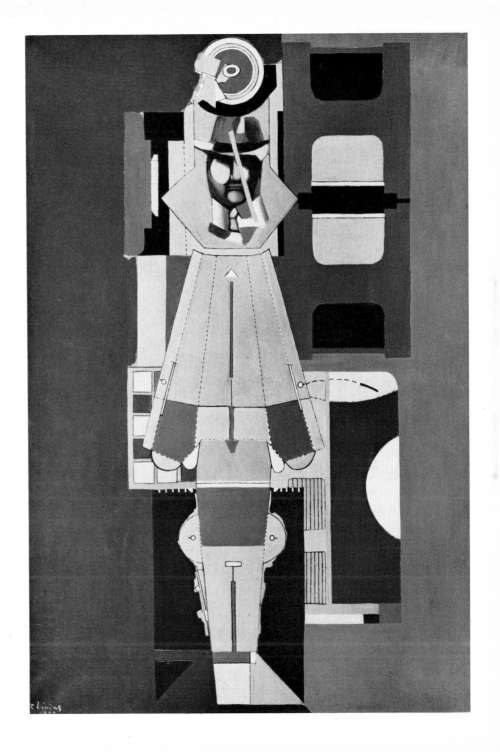

15

17

18

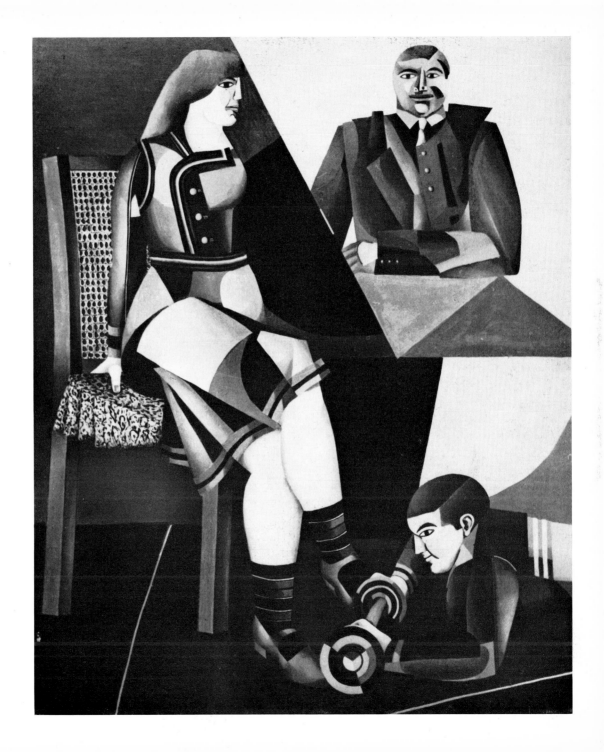

21

22

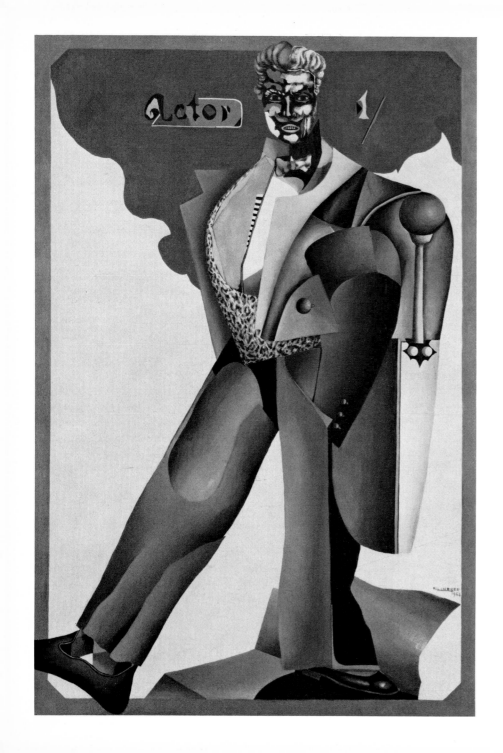

28

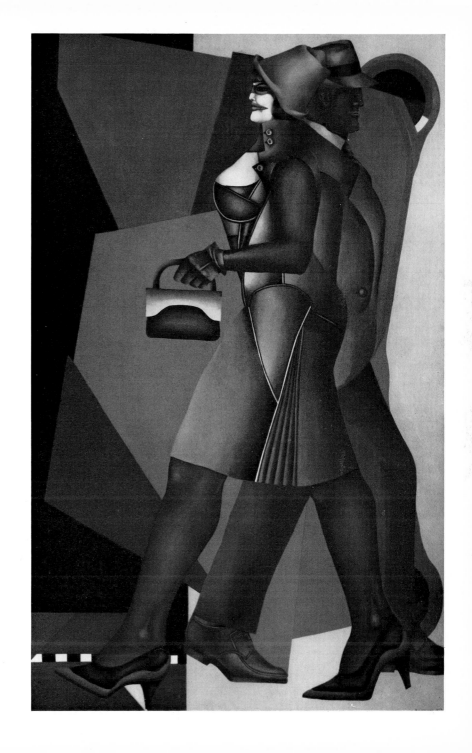

29

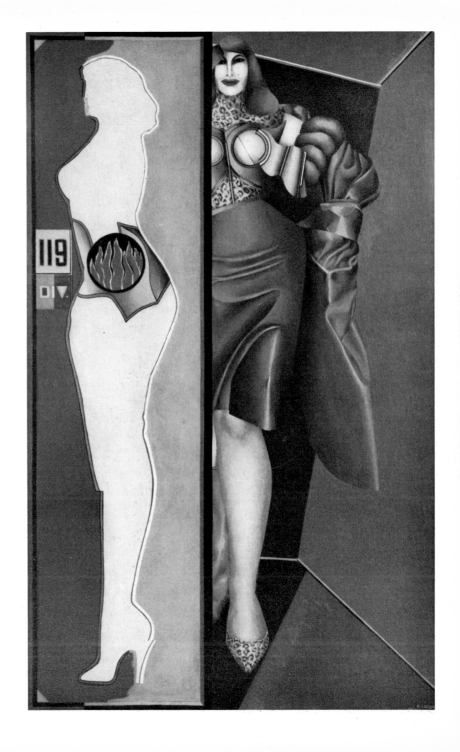

31

34

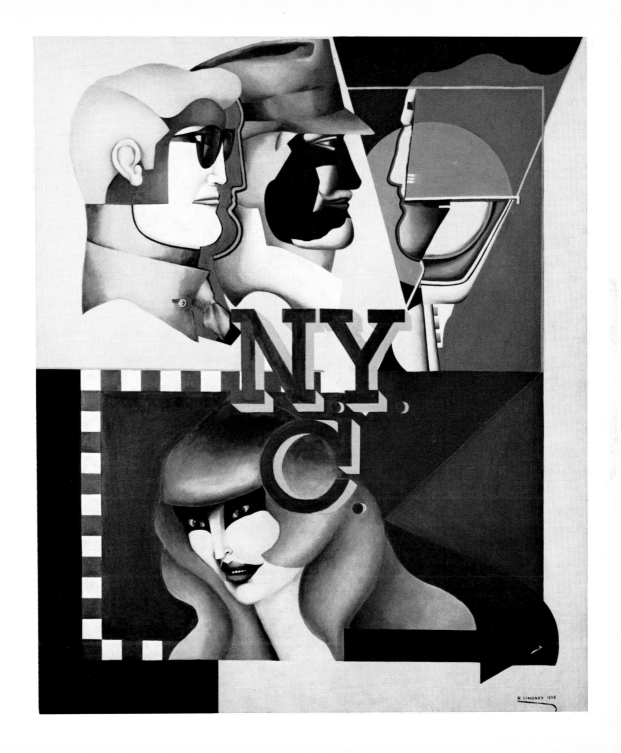

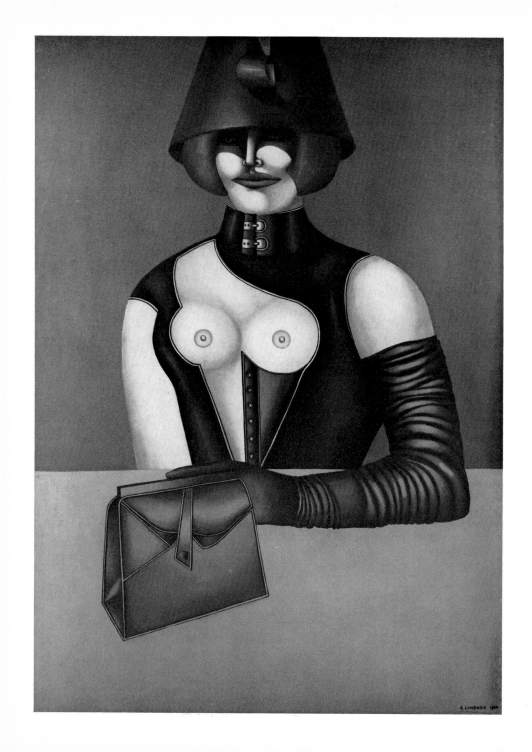

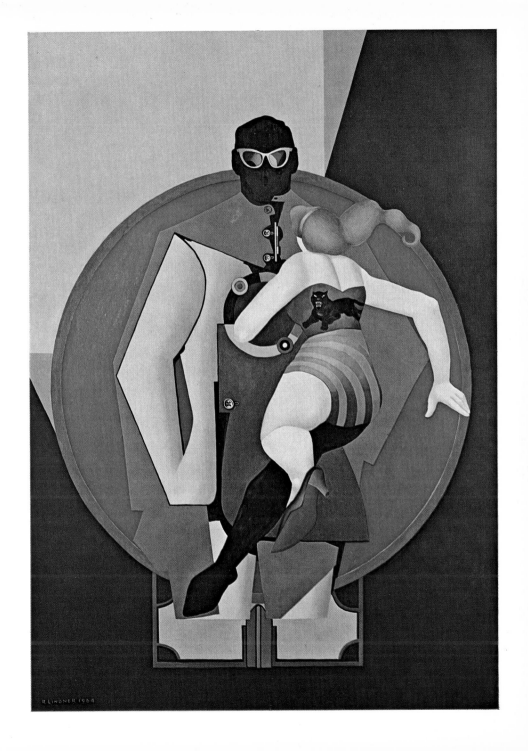

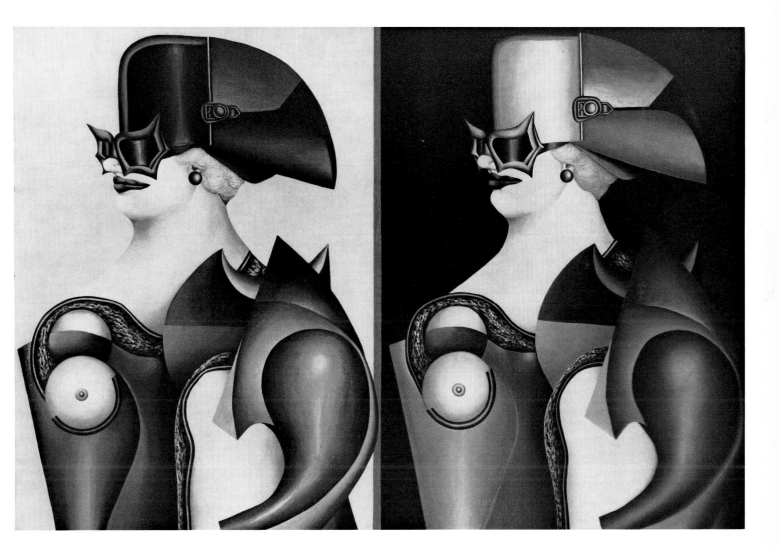

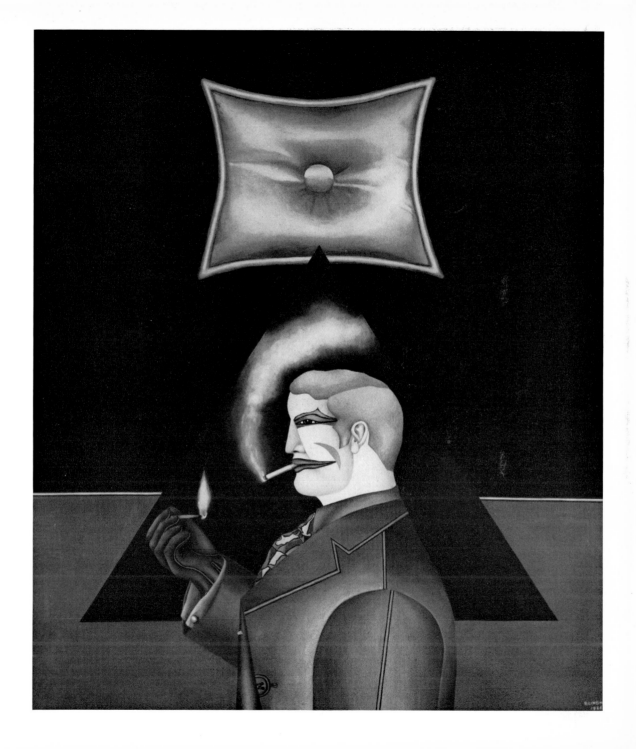

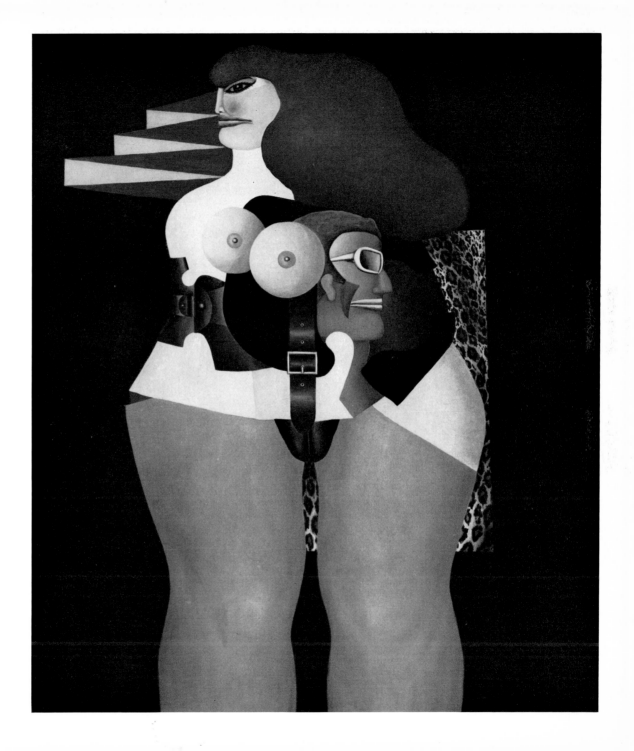

49

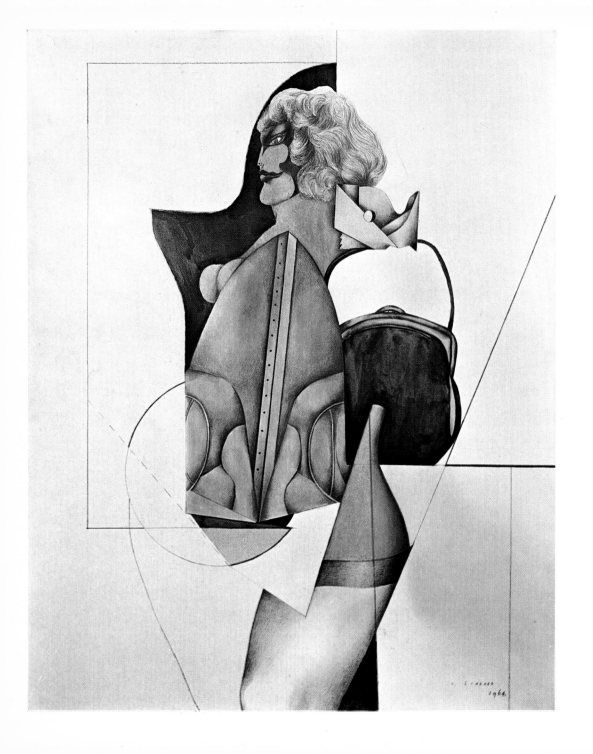

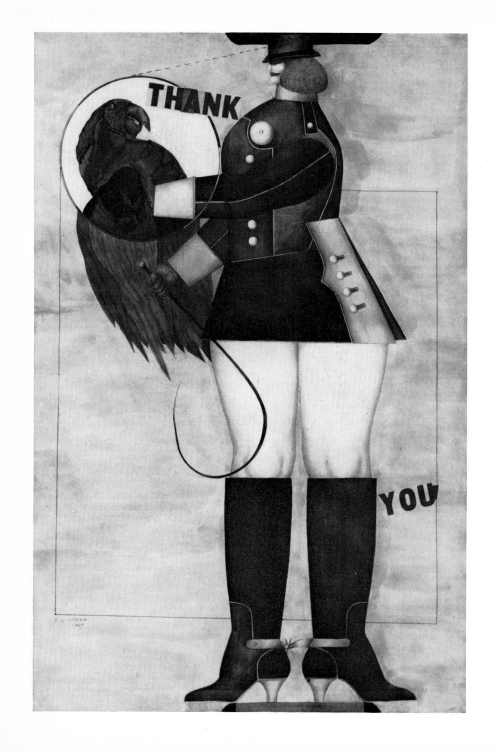

List of Plates

1   Marcel Proust, 1950
    Oil on canvas, 28 × 24″, Galerie Claude Bernard, Paris
2   The Corset, 1954
    Watercolor, 29 × 23″, B. C. Holland Gallery, Chicago
3   The Meeting, 1953
    Oil on canvas, 60 × 72″, Museum of Modern Art, New York
5   The Visitor, 1953
    Oil on canvas, 50 × 30″, Collection Miss Helen Mary Harding, New York
6   The Couple, 1955
    Oil on canvas, Collection William Copley, New York
7   Boy with Machine, 1954
    Oil on canvas, 40 × 30″, Collection Mr. and Mrs. C. L. Harrison, Batavia, Ohio
8   The Billiard, 1954/55
    Oil on canvas, 30 × 40″, Collection Mr. H. Marc Moyens, Alexandria, Virginia
9   The Couple, 1955
    Oil on canvas, 50 × 59$^3/_4$″, D. and J. de Menil Collection, Houston, Texas
10 Woman in Corset, 1956
    Oil on canvas, 25 × 18″, Cordier & Ekstrom Gallery, New York
11 The Brothers, 1958
    Oil on canvas, 39 × 25″, Private Collection
12 One Afternoon, 1958
    Oil on canvas, 40 × 30″, Cordier & Ekstrom Gallery, New York
13 Pause, 1958/61
    Oil on canvas, 50 × 35″, Cordier & Ekstrom Gallery, New York
14 The Entry, 1958
    Oil on canvas, 56 × 47″, Betty Parsons Gallery, New York
15 Stranger No. 2, 1958
    Oil on canvas, 60 × 40″, The Tate Gallery, London
17 Stranger No. 1, 1958
    Oil on canvas, 50 × 30″, Collection Mr. and Mrs. Herman H. Elkon,
    New York

18   Night Actor, 1959
Oil on canvas, 40 × 30″, B. C. Holland Gallery, Chicago, Illinois

19   The Target, 1959
Oil on canvas, 60 × 40″, Galerie Claude Bernard, Paris

20   The Secret, 1960
Oil on canvas, 50 × 40″, Collection Mr. Myron Orlofsky, White Plains, N. Y.

21   The Table, 1961
Oil on canvas, 60 × 50″, Collection Mr. and Mrs. Leonard Horwich, Chicago, Illinois

22   Two Faces, 1961
Oil on canvas, 50 × 40″, Collection Mr. Burdette S. Wright Jr., Washington

23   Musical Visit, 1961
Oil on canvas, 50 × 40″, Galerie Claude Bernard, Paris

24   Louis II, 1962
Oil on canvas, 50 × 40″, Contemporary Collection of The Cleveland Museum of Art, Cleveland, Ohio

25   Napoleon Still Life, 1962
Oil on canvas, 49$^1/_2$ × 39$^1/_2$″, Collection Mrs. René Bouche, New York

27   The Target No. 1, 1960
Oil on canvas, 60 × 40″, Cordier & Ekstrom Gallery, New York

28   The Actor, 1963
Oil on canvas, 60$^1/_4$ × 39$^3/_4$″, Collection Klaus and Helga Hegewisch, Hamburg

29   Moon Over Alabama, 1963
Oil on canvas, 80 × 40″, Collection Mr. and Mrs. Charles B. Benenson, New York

30   Solitary III, 1962
Oil on canvas, 42 × 27″, Robert Fraser Gallery, London

31   119th Division, 1963
Oil on canvas, 80 × 50″, Walker Art Center, Minneapolis

33   Coney Island, 1961
Oil on canvas, 60 × 40″, Noah Goldowsky Gallery, New York

One Man Exhibitions

1954	Betty Parsons Gallery, New York
1956	Betty Parsons Gallery, New York
1959	Betty Parsons Gallery, New York
1961	Cordier & Warren Gallery, New York
1963	Cordier & Ekstrom, Inc., New York
	Robert Fraser Gallery, London
1964	Cordier & Ekstrom, Inc., New York
1965	Cordier & Ekstrom, Inc., New York
	Galerie Claude Bernard, Paris
1966	Cordier & Ekstrom, Inc., New York
	Galleria d'Arte Contemporanea, Turin
1967	Cordier & Ekstrom, Inc., New York
1968	Städtisches Museum Schloss Morsbroich, Leverkusen
	Kestner-Gesellschaft, Hanover
1969	Staatliche Kunsthalle, Baden-Baden
	Haus am Waldsee, Berlin
	University of California, Berkeley

Richard Lindner was born in Hamburg in 1901. He began his art studies at the Kunst-gewerbeschule in Nuremberg and later attended the Kunstakademie in Munich.
Under the pressure of the Nazi regime he left Germany in 1933 and lived in Paris up to the outbreak of World War II. In March, 1941, he arrived in the United States – penniless; within a short time, however, he was earning large fees as an illustrator for such magazines as *Fortune*, *Vogue*, and *Harper's Bazaar*. He later became an instructor at Pratt Institute in Brooklyn, but resigned his post in 1965 in order to devote himself entirely to painting. Lindner now lives in New York. His work is to be found in the following museums: The Whitney Museum of American Art, New York; The Museum of Modern Art, New York; The Cleveland Museum of Art; The Walker Art Center, Minneapolis; The Dallas Museum of Fine Arts; and The Tate Gallery, London. In 1957 Lindner received a grant from the William and Noma Copley Foundation.

Bibliography

1954

First One Man Show in America at Betty Parsons Gallery, Art News, LII, February, 1954, p. 44
B. C., *Reviews and Previews*, Art News, LII, February, 1954
Emily Genauer, *In the Art Galleries*, New York Herald Tribune, January 31, 1954
Robert Rosenblum, *A Sophisticated Primitive; Exhibition at Betty Parsons Gallery*, Art Digest, XXIX, February 15, 1954, p. 13

1956

E. C. M., *Exhibition of Paintings at Betty Parsons Gallery*, Art News, LIV, February, 1956, p. 55
A. V., *Exhibition of Paintings and Drawings at Betty Parsons Gallery*, Arts, XXX, March, 1956, p. 57

1959

Dore Ashton, *Art: Gallery Exhibitions*, New York Times, February 26, 1959
Lawrence Campbell, *Exhibition at Betty Parsons Gallery*, Art News, LVII, February, 1959, p. 15
Emily Genauer, *Solo by Lindner*, New York Herald Tribune, February 21, 1959
Stuart Preston, *Shockers*, New York Times, February 22, 1959

1960

Sidney Tillim, *Lindner*. Monograph published by the William and Noma Copley Foundation, Chicago, 1960

1961

Exhibition at Cordier & Warren, Art News, LX, October, 1961, p. 10–11
Sidney Tillim, *John Graham and Richard Lindner*, Arts, XXXVI, November, 1961, p. 34–37

1962

Art International, VI, 7, September, 1962, p. 37
Dore Ashton, *Art U. S. A. 1962*, Studio, CLXIII, March, 1962, p. 91
Dore Ashton, *Exhibition at Cordier & Warren*, Arts and Architecture, LXXIX, February, 1962, p. 6
George Butcher, *Striven Identity*, The Guardian, July 11, 1962, p. 5
Robert Melville, *First London Exhibition*, The Architectural Review, CXXXII, November, 1962, p. 363
Mr. Lindner's Paintings, The Times (London), June 25, 1962
Jasia Reichardt, *Les Expositions à l'étranger: Londres*, Aujourd'hui, VI, September, 1962, p. 58
Colette Roberts, *Lettre de New York*, Aujourd'hui, VI, September, 1962, p. 61
Irving Sandler, *In the Art Galleries*, New York Post, June 17, 1962
Michael Shepherd, The Arts Review, June 16–30, 1962
Sidney Tillim, *Richard Lindner*, Aujourd'hui, VI, February, 1962, p. 26–29
G. S. Whittet, Studio, CLXIV, September, 1962, p. 116

1963

Dore Ashton, *Americans at the Museum of Modern Art*, Arts and Architecture, LXXX, July, 1963, p. 4
Gene Baro, *Gathering of Americans*, Arts, XXXVII, September, 1963, p. 33

Thomas B. Hess, *Phony Crisis in American Art*, Art News, LXII, Summer, 1963, p. 28

Jules Langsner, *Los Angeles Letter*, Art International, VII, 6, June, 1963, p. 77

Richard Lindner, *Statement*, Catalogue "Americans 1963", Museum of Modern Art, New York

Dorothy G. Seckler, *The Artist in America: Victim of the Cultural Boom?*, Art in America, LI, 6, December, 1963, p. 28–39

1964

Dore Ashton, *Die Zeichnung in der modernen amerikanischen Kunst*, Catalogue "I. Internationale der Zeichnung", Darmstadt, November, 1964, p. 29–43

Dore Ashton, *Richard Lindner, the Secret of the Inner Voice*, Studio, CLXVII, January, 1964, p. 12–17

S. G., *Exhibition at Cordier & Ekstrom*, Art News, LXIII, March, 1964, p. 10

E. T. Kelly, *Neo-Dada; a Critique of Pop Art*, Art Journal, XXIII, 3, Spring, 1964, p. 200

James Monte, *Americans 1963, San Francisco Museum of Art*, Art Forum, III, 1, September, 1964, p. 43–44

Brian O'Doherty, *Lindner's Private but very Modern Hades*, New York Times, March 8, 1964

Painter of the Crass Crowd, Time Magazine, LXXXIII, March 20, 1964, p. 70

Vivian Raynor, *Exhibition at Cordier & Ekstrom*, Arts, XXXVIII, May, 1964, p. 41

Colette Roberts, *Les Expositions à New York*, Aujourd'hui, VIII, January, 1964, p. 96

Stop, Caution, Go, Newsweek, LXIII, March 9, 1964, p. 53

Charlotte Willard, *Drawing Today*, Art in America, LII, October, 1964, p. 64

1965

Rolf-Gunter Dienst, *Richard Lindner*, Das Kunstwerk, XIX, 2, August, 1965, p. 21

N. E., *Collages and Paintings at Cordier & Ekstrom*, Art News, LXIV, April, 1965, p. 11

Exhibition at Cordier & Ekstrom, Time Magazine, February 26, 1965

Flags, New Glories, Time Magazine, April 9, 1965

Simone Frigerio, *Exposition à la Galerie Claude Bernard*, Aujourd'hui, IX, July, 1965, p. 87

John Gruen, *Three Old Masters*, New York Herald Tribune, February, 1965, p. 28

Jean-Jacques Levêque, *Richard Lindner*, La Nouvelle Revue Française, XIII, 154, October, 1965, p. 735–36

Richard Lindner, *Statement*, Art Voices, Fall, 1965, p. 64

Stuart Preston, *Art: Hans Hofmann at a Vigorous 85*, New York Times, February 20, 1965, p. 22

N. Rosenthal, *Six Day Bicycle Wheel Race: Multiple Originals*, Art in America, LIII, October, 1965, p. 101

Franz Schulz, *The Corcoran's American Mixture, 1965*, New York Times, February 28, 1965

G. Stiles, *Exhibition at Cordier & Ekstrom*, Arts, XXXIX, April, 1965, p. 65

1966

Eros in Polyester, Newsweek, October 10, 1966

John Gruen, *The Art of Cruelty*, New York World Journal Tribune, New York Magazine, October, 1966

E. B. Henning, *German Expressionist Paintings at the Cleveland Museum of Art*, Burlington Magazine, CVIII, December, 1966, p. 632–633

Portrait, Das Kunstwerk, XIX, April, 1966, p. 109

1967

Artists: Beal Booster, Time Magazine, February 3, 1967, p. 44

Dore Ashton, *Exhibition at Cordier & Ekstrom*, Arts and Architecture, LXXXIV, March, 1967, p. 4

Dore Ashton, *Exhibition at Cordier & Ekstrom*, Studio, CLXXIII, March, 1967, p. 153

Dore Ashton, *New York Gallery Notes: Show at Cordier & Ekstrom*, Art in America, LV, January, 1967, p. 90

Rolf-Gunter Dienst, *Richard Lindner*, Das Kunstwerk, XX, February, 1967, p. 22–26

Grace Glueck, *Art Notes: Macy's is his Louvre*, New York Times, January 15, 1967

John Gruen, *Richard Lindner's Nightmare Women*, New York World Journal Tribune, January 15, 1967, p. 26–27

Hilton Kramer, *Richard Lindner: A Dream of Decadent Vitality*, New York Times, January 22, 1967, p. 25

Roland Penrose, *Richard Lindner*, Art International, XI, 1, January 20, 1967, p. 30–32

John Perreault, *Venus in Vinyl*, Art News, LXV, January, 1967, p. 46–48

Lil Picard, *The Turn of the Brush*, East Village Other, II, 4, January 15–February 1, 1967, p. 14

1968

Rolf-Gunter Dienst, *Positionen*, Cologne, DuMont-Schauberg, 1968, p. 69–72

Rolf-Gunter Dienst, *Graphic USA*, Baden-Baden, Edition Plus, 1968